Your Path to Financial Independence

A Comprehensive Guide to Attaining Prosperity and Pleasure

Profitable Man

Table of Contents

Introduction to the 5 Journeyer Stages: Understanding Your Financial Journeyer Stage

Embarking on the path to financial independence is not a one-size-fits-all journey; it's a dynamic process that evolves over time. In the opening chapter of "Your Path to Financial Independence," Jamila Souffrant lays the foundation by introducing readers to the crucial concept of the 5 Journeyer Stages. These stages serve as a compass, guiding individuals through the intricate terrain of personal finance and helping them understand where they stand in their pursuit of financial freedom.

1.1 Introduction to the 5 Journeyer Stages:

The initial section of this chapter delves into the significance of the 5 Journeyer Stages, each representing a distinct phase in an individual's financial life. Souffrant recognizes that everyone's financial journey is unique, influenced by factors such as income, lifestyle choices, and personal goals. By categorizing these stages, readers gain a valuable framework to assess their current financial position and set realistic expectations for the future.

1.2 Assessing Your Current Financial Stage:

Building on the foundation of the Journeyer Stages, Souffrant guides readers through a self-assessment process. This involves evaluating various aspects of their financial standing, including income, expenses, assets, and debts. Through insightful questions and practical exercises, readers gain a deeper understanding of their current financial stage and the key areas that demand attention.

1.3 Setting Spending and Saving Goals Based on Your Journeyer Stage:

Once individuals have identified their current Journeyer Stage, the chapter progresses to the essential task of aligning spending and saving goals accordingly. Souffrant emphasizes the importance of setting realistic and achievable objectives, taking into account the unique challenges and opportunities presented by each stage. Readers learn to tailor their financial plans to suit their specific circumstances, fostering a sense of empowerment and control over their economic destiny.

This chapter serves as a crucial starting point for readers, laying the groundwork for the transformative journey ahead. By embracing the concept of the 5 Journeyer Stages, individuals gain a newfound perspective on their financial landscape, enabling them to make informed decisions that align with their goals. As readers delve into the subsequent chapters, they carry with them the valuable insights gained from understanding their current financial stage—a cornerstone in the quest for prosperity and pleasure.

In the intricate tapestry of personal finance, one's journey to financial independence is inherently dynamic and diverse. In the second section of "Your Path to Financial Independence," Jamila Souffrant intricately explores the pivotal aspect of assessing one's current financial stage. This introspective process acts as a compass, guiding individuals through the labyrinth of income, expenses, assets, and debts to gain a comprehensive understanding of their financial standing.

2.1 The Significance of Self-Assessment:

The journey to financial independence begins with self-awareness. Souffrant underscores the importance of assessing one's current financial stage as a fundamental step in crafting a personalized roadmap to prosperity. This process is not merely about numbers; it's about gaining insight into one's financial habits, lifestyle choices, and long-term aspirations. By delving into the intricacies of personal finance, individuals can make informed decisions that resonate with their unique circumstances.

2.2 Evaluating Key Financial Metrics:

The chapter unfolds with a detailed exploration of the key metrics that define one's financial stage. Readers are encouraged to scrutinize their income sources, analyze their spending patterns, take stock of existing assets, and confront any outstanding debts. Souffrant employs a holistic approach, recognizing that financial well-being encompasses more than just the balance in a bank account. It involves a nuanced understanding of how various financial elements interconnect to shape an individual's overall economic health.

2.3 Identifying Strengths and Areas for Improvement:

Self-assessment is not about judgment; it is about empowerment. Souffrant guides readers in recognizing their financial strengths and applauding responsible money management. Simultaneously, the chapter encourages an honest confrontation with areas that may need improvement. Whether it's curbing unnecessary expenses, exploring additional income streams, or addressing outstanding debts, this introspective process paves the way for constructive and actionable insights.

Armed with a nuanced understanding of their current financial stage, readers emerge equipped with a personalized financial portrait. This awareness empowers them to set realistic goals, make informed financial decisions, and navigate the subsequent stages of their journey to financial independence with confidence. Souffrant's approach goes beyond mere numerical analysis; it invites readers to engage in a profound exploration of their relationship with money, fostering a sense of financial autonomy that is both liberating and transformative. As individuals progress through this chapter, they lay the groundwork for a more intentional and purposeful financial future.

CHAPTER TWO

In the exploration of personal finance, the concept of financial independence and early retirement emerges as a beacon of liberation and empowerment. Within the pages of "Your Path to Financial Independence," Jamila Souffrant meticulously navigates readers through the transformative landscape of these ideals, providing a roadmap to understand, define, and ultimately achieve financial independence and early retirement.

2.1 Unraveling the Notion of Financial Independence:

The journey begins with a comprehensive examination of what financial independence truly means. Souffrant demystifies the term, transcending the simplistic notion of wealth accumulation. Financial independence, as portrayed in this chapter, is about attaining a state where an individual's passive income is sufficient to cover their living expenses, freeing them from the constraints of traditional employment. The author emphasizes the importance of aligning financial goals with personal values and aspirations, crafting a nuanced and individualized definition of financial independence.

2.2 Early Retirement as a Strategic Goal:

Building upon the foundation of financial independence, Souffrant introduces the concept of early retirement. Early retirement, in this context, is not merely an escape from work but a strategic goal to achieve financial freedom ahead of traditional retirement age. The chapter delves into the benefits and challenges of early retirement, encouraging readers to envision a life where their time is no longer tethered to the demands of a 9-to-5 job. Souffrant expertly explores the emotional and psychological aspects of early retirement, fostering a holistic understanding of its implications on lifestyle and well-being.

2.3 Crafting a Personalized Plan for Financial Freedom:

With the definitions established, the chapter unfolds into the practicalities of mapping out a personalized plan for financial independence. Souffrant guides readers through the process of setting actionable goals, understanding their risk tolerance, and building a diversified investment portfolio. The emphasis is on creating a robust financial foundation that aligns with individual circumstances and aspirations. Through engaging narratives and real-world examples, readers are inspired to envision their unique path to financial freedom.

This chapter is not a mere guide; it is an invitation to reimagine one's relationship with money and work. By defining financial independence and early retirement in a personalized context, Souffrant empowers readers to break free from conventional financial norms and pave their own way to a fulfilling and liberated future. As individuals engage with the insights and strategies presented in this chapter, they embark on a journey that transcends financial goals—it becomes a journey of self-discovery, purposeful living, and the pursuit of a life truly aligned with one's deepest values.

In the expansive landscape of personal finance, the notion of quitting one's job and retiring early stands as a compelling and transformative goal. Within the pages of "Your Path to Financial Independence," Jamila Souffrant intricately navigates readers through the diverse scenarios that encompass this dream, offering practical insights and strategic considerations to facilitate a seamless transition towards early retirement.

2.1 The Allure of Early Retirement:

The chapter unfolds by delving into the allure of early retirement, exploring the motivations and aspirations that drive individuals to contemplate stepping away from traditional employment ahead of schedule. Souffrant's narrative extends beyond financial considerations, acknowledging the desire for increased autonomy, enhanced life experiences, and the pursuit of personal passions. By framing early retirement as a lifestyle choice rather than a mere financial decision, readers are encouraged to envision a future that transcends the conventional boundaries of work.

2.2 Calculating the Financial Numbers:

Practicality merges with aspiration as Souffrant guides readers through the crucial task of calculating the financial numbers required for early retirement. From estimating living expenses and projecting inflation to determining the needed savings and investment portfolios, this section provides a comprehensive overview of the quantitative aspects that underpin a successful early retirement plan. Real-life case studies and scenarios offer readers tangible examples, allowing them to see how the numbers align with their individual goals.

2.3 Navigating Different Scenarios:

Not all early retirements are created equal, and Souffrant recognizes this diversity by presenting readers with a spectrum of scenarios. Whether it's the entrepreneurially spirited individual eager to start a passion project, the minimalist seeking a frugal and intentional lifestyle, or the adventurer looking to explore the world, the chapter explores how various scenarios cater to different personalities and objectives. Souffrant offers valuable insights into tailoring an early retirement plan that aligns with individual preferences, making the dream of quitting the nine-to-five a tangible and customized reality.

2.4 Mitigating Risks and Challenges:

While early retirement carries the promise of freedom, it is not without its challenges. Souffrant addresses potential risks and pitfalls that individuals may encounter during their journey. From market fluctuations and unexpected expenses to the psychological adjustments of transitioning from a structured work routine to newfound freedom, readers gain a well-rounded understanding of the complexities involved. The chapter equips them with strategies to mitigate risks, ensuring a more resilient and secure path to early retirement.

By the end of this chapter, readers are not only armed with the financial acumen necessary for early retirement but are also enriched with a profound appreciation for the diversity of scenarios that this lifestyle transition can encompass. Souffrant's approach transcends the traditional financial guide, offering readers a holistic perspective that integrates financial prudence with the pursuit of personal fulfillment and purpose. The chapter serves as a compass, guiding readers through the intricate decision-making process of quitting their job and retiring early, ultimately enabling them to craft a life that aligns with their deepest aspirations.

In the pursuit of financial independence, the journey is not only about reaching a numerical milestone but also about crafting a personalized and sustainable plan that aligns with one's unique goals and values. Within the pages of "Your Path to Financial Independence," Jamila Souffrant meticulously guides readers through the intricate process of crafting a personalized plan for financial freedom, offering a roadmap that extends beyond generic advice to address individual circumstances and aspirations.

3.1 Setting Actionable Goals:

The chapter begins with the fundamental step of setting actionable goals. Souffrant underscores the importance of specificity and realism in goal-setting, urging readers to move beyond vague aspirations and define tangible objectives. Whether it's paying off a specific amount of debt, saving for a dream home, or achieving a targeted level of passive income, the author emphasizes the transformative power of clear and measurable goals in driving financial progress.

3.2 Understanding Risk Tolerance:

Recognizing that every individual's relationship with risk is unique, Souffrant delves into the concept of risk tolerance. Understanding how comfortable one is with financial risks is crucial in developing an investment strategy that aligns with their personality and financial objectives. Through insightful self-reflection and practical exercises, readers gain a nuanced understanding of their risk tolerance, laying the groundwork for a well-balanced and personalized financial plan.

3.3 Building a Diversified Investment Portfolio:

The chapter navigates into the realm of investments, emphasizing the importance of a diversified portfolio tailored to individual goals and risk tolerance. Souffrant demystifies investment concepts, making them accessible to readers at various levels of financial literacy. From stocks and bonds to real estate and alternative investments, the author provides a comprehensive overview, empowering readers to make informed decisions that align with their financial objectives and timeline.

3.4 Navigating Tax Strategies and Financial Tools:

Beyond investments, Souffrant guides readers through the often-overlooked terrain of tax strategies and financial tools. Understanding how to optimize tax efficiency and leverage financial tools can significantly impact the growth of wealth. This section equips readers with the knowledge to make strategic decisions around tax planning, retirement accounts, and other financial instruments that can enhance their journey towards financial freedom.

3.5 Embracing Flexibility and Adaptability:

Recognizing the dynamic nature of life and financial markets, Souffrant encourages readers to embrace flexibility and adaptability in their financial plans. Unexpected events, market fluctuations, and personal life changes are inevitable, and a successful financial plan should be resilient enough to withstand these challenges. The chapter provides guidance on regularly reviewing and adjusting the financial plan to ensure it remains relevant and effective over time.

In conclusion, "Crafting a Personalized Plan for Financial Freedom" serves as a pivotal chapter in the journey towards financial independence.

Souffrant's approach goes beyond generic financial advice, recognizing the individuality of each reader's circumstances. By empowering readers to set actionable goals, understand their risk tolerance, build a diversified investment portfolio, navigate tax strategies, and embrace flexibility, the chapter provides a comprehensive toolkit for crafting a financial plan that is not only effective but also aligned with one's unique aspirations. As readers engage with the insights and strategies presented, they are equipped to navigate the complexities of financial planning with confidence and purpose, ultimately paving the way for a future defined by financial freedom and fulfillment.

CHAPTER THREE

In the pursuit of financial independence, the way we manage our daily expenses holds the key to unlocking a more intentional and joyful life. Jamila Souffrant, in her insightful guide "Your Path to Financial Independence," dedicates an entire chapter to the critical task of reevaluating daily expenditures and pinpointing costly habits. The chapter, aptly titled "Balancing Expenses for Joyful Living," invites readers to reconsider their relationship with money and expenditures, providing a roadmap for cultivating financial wellness without sacrificing the joys of life.

3.1 Challenging Conventional Spending Habits:

The journey begins by challenging conventional spending habits. Souffrant prompts readers to scrutinize their daily expenses and question the necessity of each financial transaction. By fostering a mindset of conscious spending, individuals can identify areas where money may be leaking unnecessarily. This section encourages a shift from mindless consumption to mindful decision-making, setting the stage for a more deliberate and fulfilling financial journey.

3.2 Identifying Costly Daily Habits:

Building on the foundation of conscious spending, the chapter dives into the specific task of identifying costly daily habits. Souffrant employs practical exercises and relatable examples to help readers pinpoint areas where their money is disproportionately allocated without bringing proportional joy or value. Whether it's habitual coffee shop visits, impulsive online shopping, or dining out excessively, readers gain insights into their spending patterns and the potential impact on their overall financial well-being.

3.3 Downsizing Strategies for Daily Costs:

With a clear understanding of spending habits, Souffrant introduces downsizing strategies to trim unnecessary daily expenses. From brewing coffee at home and embracing a minimalist wardrobe to exploring budget-friendly alternatives for leisure activities, readers discover practical and actionable steps to optimize their daily expenditures. The author emphasizes that small, intentional changes in daily habits can cumulatively contribute to significant financial progress over time.

3.4 Allocating Budget for Joyful Expenditures:

The chapter strikes a delicate balance by acknowledging that financial well-being should not come at the expense of joy and fulfillment. Souffrant encourages readers to allocate a portion of their budget for expenses that genuinely bring joy and satisfaction. This intentional approach to budgeting allows individuals to indulge in activities and experiences that contribute to their overall well-being without compromising their long-term financial goals.

3.5 Cultivating a Mindful and Joyful Spending Mindset:

Ultimately, "Balancing Expenses for Joyful Living" seeks to cultivate a mindful and joyful spending mindset. Souffrant advocates for a shift from deprivation to empowerment, where individuals actively choose how and where to allocate their resources based on their values and priorities. By aligning spending decisions with personal joy and fulfillment, readers can create a financial plan that not only supports their long-term goals but also enhances their day-to-day quality of life.

As readers engage with this chapter, they embark on a transformative journey of reevaluating their daily expenses and identifying costly habits. Souffrant's approach goes beyond traditional budgeting advice; it invites readers to infuse intentionality and joy into their financial decisions. By striking a harmonious balance between responsible spending and joyful living, individuals lay the foundation for a sustainable and fulfilling financial future. "Balancing Expenses for Joyful Living" becomes a guiding beacon, illuminating the path toward financial independence without sacrificing the pleasures that make life truly meaningful.

4.1 Embracing the Power of Mindful Consumption:

The journey into downsizing begins with a fundamental shift in mindset — from unconscious consumption to mindful living. Souffrant advocates for a heightened awareness of the choices individuals make in their daily lives, urging readers to consider the impact of each expenditure on their financial health and, equally important, on their happiness. This mindset shift lays the groundwork for a more intentional approach to daily expenses.

4.2 Brewing Your Own Financial Freedom:

The daily ritual of grabbing a cup of coffee on the way to work might seem innocuous, but it can add up to a significant chunk of monthly expenses. Souffrant explores the idea of brewing financial freedom by encouraging readers to revisit their coffee habits. Practical strategies, such as investing in a quality coffee maker or exploring cost-effective alternatives, empower individuals to enjoy their favorite beverage without draining their wallets.

4.3 The Wardrobe Revolution:

The allure of a stylish wardrobe often leads to unnecessary spending. Souffrant prompts readers to embark on a wardrobe revolution by reconsidering their clothing habits. Strategies like embracing a minimalist wardrobe, exploring second-hand options, and focusing on versatile pieces contribute not only to financial savings but also to a more sustainable and conscious approach to fashion.

4.4 Budget-Friendly Alternatives for Leisure Activities:

Leisure activities play a vital role in overall well-being, but they need not come with a hefty price tag. Souffrant introduces readers to budget-friendly alternatives for entertainment and relaxation, from exploring local parks and free community events to embracing the benefits of at-home leisure. These downsizing strategies empower individuals to enjoy life's pleasures without sacrificing financial stability.

4.5 Transforming Mealtime into a Feast of Savings:

Daily dining expenses can quickly accumulate, but Souffrant offers transformative strategies to turn mealtime into a feast of savings. Whether it's embracing home-cooked meals, meal prepping to avoid impulsive restaurant visits, or exploring cost-effective grocery shopping, readers learn to savor the joy of good food without overspending.

4.6 Prioritizing Experiences Over Possessions:

The chapter concludes with a profound exploration of the shift from possession-centric to experience-centric living. Souffrant advocates for prioritizing experiences that bring lasting joy and fulfillment, emphasizing that meaningful memories often surpass the temporary satisfaction derived from material possessions. By focusing on experiences, individuals not only enhance their quality of life but also naturally reduce unnecessary daily costs.

In essence, "Downsizing Strategies for Daily Costs" emerges as a practical and empowering guide within the broader context of financial independence. Souffrant's approach transcends mere budgeting advice; it invites readers to embark on a journey of intentional living. By implementing strategic downsizing measures, individuals can align their daily expenses with their values, fostering a sense of financial freedom and joy. This chapter serves as a compass, navigating the delicate balance between financial responsibility and the pursuit of a rich and meaningful life. As readers engage with the downsizing strategies presented, they gain not only financial resilience but also a profound appreciation for the simplicity and joy that can be found in mindful and intentional daily living.

Allocating Budget for Joyful Expenditures, Including That Extra Side of Guacamole: Balancing Expenses for Joyful Living

In the intricate tapestry of financial planning, the chapter on "Allocating Budget for Joyful Expenditures" in Jamila Souffrant's "Your Path to Financial Independence" stands as a beacon, guiding readers to strike a harmonious balance between fiscal responsibility and the pursuit of joy. This segment of the guide serves as an invitation to reimagine budgeting not as a restrictive measure but as a tool for intentional living, allowing individuals to allocate resources for experiences and indulgences that bring genuine happiness.

5.1 Redefining Budgeting as a Tool for Joyful Living:

The chapter commences by challenging conventional perceptions of budgeting as a restrictive and rigid practice. Souffrant encourages readers to view budgeting as a dynamic tool that can be tailored to prioritize joy and fulfillment. By redefining the purpose of budgeting, individuals can liberate themselves from financial constraints while still working towards long-term goals.

5.2 Identifying Joyful Expenditures:

A pivotal aspect of this chapter lies in the exploration of joyful expenditures. Souffrant prompts readers to reflect on the activities, experiences, and items that genuinely bring them happiness. Whether it's a favorite hobby, a special dining experience, or the seemingly indulgent extra side of guacamole, readers are encouraged to identify and embrace those joyful moments that make life rich and fulfilling.

5.3 Creating a Joyful Expenditure Category in the Budget:

The practical application of this philosophy involves the creation of a dedicated category in the budget for joyful expenditures. Souffrant guides readers through the process of allocating a portion of their income specifically for activities and items that contribute to their well-being and happiness. This intentional budgeting approach allows individuals to enjoy guilty pleasures, such as that extra side of guacamole, without jeopardizing their overall financial health.

5.4 Balancing Joyful Spending with Long-Term Goals:

While embracing joyful expenditures, Souffrant underscores the importance of maintaining a delicate balance with long-term financial goals. The chapter provides insights into strategic budgeting, ensuring that the pursuit of joy does not compromise the overarching objective of financial independence. Readers learn to allocate resources wisely, ensuring that both immediate pleasures and future aspirations are considered in the budgeting process.

5.5 The Psychological Impact of Joyful Expenditures:

Beyond the financial aspects, the chapter explores the psychological impact of incorporating joyful expenditures into the budget. Souffrant delves into the importance of cultivating a positive relationship with money and how intentional spending on things that bring joy contributes to overall life satisfaction. By aligning expenditures with personal values, individuals can experience a profound sense of fulfillment and purpose in their financial journey.

5.6 Cultivating a Mindful Approach to Joyful Living:

Ultimately, the chapter encourages readers to cultivate a mindful approach to joyful living. Souffrant's philosophy transcends traditional financial advice, guiding individuals to not only manage their money wisely but to infuse each financial decision with intentionality and purpose. By embracing joyful expenditures in the budget, individuals can craft a lifestyle that is both financially sustainable and deeply satisfying.

In essence, "Allocating Budget for Joyful Expenditures, Including That Extra Side of Guacamole" is a transformative chapter that transcends the conventional boundaries of budgeting. Souffrant's approach serves as a roadmap for individuals to navigate the delicate balance between responsible financial management and the pursuit of a joyful and fulfilling life. By creating space in the budget for activities and items that spark joy, readers can savor the richness of life without sacrificing long-term financial well-being. This chapter serves as a guide, encouraging individuals to view budgeting not as a constraint but as a powerful tool for intentional and joyful living. As readers engage with the insights and strategies presented, they embark on a journey that celebrates the joy found in both the small pleasures and the long-term aspirations of life.

CHAPTER FOUR

Understanding the Impact of Debt on Your Financial
Independence: Mastering Debt Payoff

Debt, often considered a necessary evil in modern financial landscapes, can exert a profound influence on an individual's journey toward financial independence. In the illuminating chapter titled "Understanding the Impact of Debt on Your Financial Independence: Mastering Debt Payoff" from Jamila Souffrant's "Your Path to Financial Independence," readers are guided through a comprehensive exploration of the intricacies surrounding debt and equipped with strategic insights on how to navigate its impact on their financial freedom.

6.1 Unveiling the Complex Dynamics of Debt:

The chapter unfolds by demystifying the complex dynamics of debt, acknowledging its multifaceted impact on one's financial well-being. Souffrant delves into various forms of debt, from credit cards and student loans to mortgages, providing readers with a nuanced understanding of how different types of debt can shape financial circumstances. By unraveling the layers of debt, readers are empowered to make informed decisions about their financial strategies.

6.2 Debt as a Barrier to Financial Independence:

A critical theme explored is the role of debt as a potential barrier to achieving financial independence. Souffrant emphasizes that while some types of debt may serve as investments in future wealth, excessive and high-interest debt can hinder progress toward financial freedom. Readers gain insights into distinguishing between "good" and "bad" debt and are guided on the strategic management of debts that align with their broader financial goals.

6.3 Assessing the Emotional Toll of Debt:

Beyond the financial implications, Souffrant addresses the emotional toll of debt. Debt can often evoke stress, anxiety, and a sense of entrapment. By acknowledging the emotional impact, readers are encouraged to approach debt payoff not just as a numerical task but as a holistic journey toward financial and emotional liberation. Souffrant provides practical tips for managing the emotional aspects of debt, fostering a healthier mindset during the debt payoff process.

6.4 Crafting an Effective Debt Payoff Plan:

The heart of the chapter lies in the strategic crafting of an effective debt payoff plan. Souffrant introduces readers to actionable steps for organizing and prioritizing debts, exploring methods like the debt snowball and debt avalanche. Through real-world examples and relatable scenarios, readers learn to tailor a debt payoff plan that aligns with their unique financial circumstances, fostering a sense of control and empowerment.

6.5 Integrating Debt Payoff with Long-Term Goals:

Recognizing that debt payoff is not an isolated task but an integral part of a broader financial strategy, Souffrant guides readers on integrating debt payoff with long-term goals. Whether it's saving for retirement, building an emergency fund, or investing in personal development, readers gain insights into aligning debt payoff efforts with their overarching aspirations, ensuring a holistic and sustainable approach to financial independence.

6.6 Celebrating Milestones and Progress:

The chapter concludes with a focus on celebrating milestones and progress in the debt payoff journey. Souffrant acknowledges that tackling debt can be a challenging endeavor, and recognizing achievements along the way is crucial for maintaining motivation. By instilling a sense of accomplishment and empowerment, readers are motivated to persevere in their journey towards debt freedom and, ultimately, financial independence.

In essence, "Understanding the Impact of Debt on Your Financial Independence: Mastering Debt Payoff" serves as a compass, guiding readers through the intricate terrain of debt management. Souffrant's approach is both pragmatic and empathetic, recognizing the multifaceted nature of debt and providing readers with the tools to navigate its impact effectively. As readers engage with the insights and strategies presented, they embark on a transformative journey toward debt freedom, paving the way for enhanced financial well-being and a clearer path to achieving true financial independence.

In the labyrinth of personal finance, the task of repaying debts can be a daunting challenge, casting a shadow on the pursuit of financial independence. Jamila Souffrant, in her enlightening guide "Your Path to Financial Independence," dedicates a crucial chapter to the art and science of debt management titled "Creating an Effective Debt Payoff Plan: Mastering Debt Payoff." This chapter serves as a comprehensive roadmap, guiding readers through the intricacies of crafting a tailored and effective strategy for liberating themselves from the shackles of debt.

7.1 Acknowledging the Debt Landscape:

The journey begins with a deep dive into the varied landscape of debt. Souffrant encourages readers to confront their debts head-on, acknowledging the specific types, amounts, and interest rates associated with each. By fostering a clear understanding of the debt landscape, individuals can lay the groundwork for a targeted and efficient debt payoff plan.

7.2 Organizing and Prioritizing Debts:

A critical step in creating an effective debt payoff plan is the organization and prioritization of debts. Souffrant introduces readers to methodologies like the debt snowball and debt avalanche, empowering them to choose an approach that aligns with their financial goals and psychological preferences. This strategic organization ensures that the debt payoff journey is not only effective but also psychologically sustainable.

7.3 Budgeting for Debt Repayment:

Central to any debt payoff plan is the integration of a realistic and sustainable budget. Souffrant guides readers through the process of budgeting for debt repayment, ensuring that each dollar is allocated purposefully toward both necessary expenses and debt obligations. The chapter provides practical tips for identifying areas where expenses can be trimmed to accelerate debt repayment without sacrificing essential needs.

7.4 Exploring Additional Income Streams:

Recognizing that increasing income can expedite the debt payoff journey, Souffrant explores the concept of additional income streams. Whether through side hustles, freelancing, or exploring entrepreneurial ventures, readers are encouraged to consider creative ways to supplement their primary income. This not only accelerates debt repayment but also cultivates a mindset of financial resourcefulness.

7.5 Negotiating Terms and Interest Rates:

A savvy debt payoff plan includes the strategic negotiation of terms and interest rates. Souffrant provides insights into approaching creditors to discuss potential adjustments to repayment terms or interest rates. This proactive approach empowers individuals to take control of their debt obligations, potentially reducing the overall cost of repayment and hastening the path to financial freedom.

7.6 Cultivating Patience and Persistence:

The chapter concludes with a crucial emphasis on the virtues of patience and persistence. Souffrant recognizes that the journey to debt freedom is a marathon, not a sprint. By cultivating a mindset of perseverance and acknowledging the small victories along the way, individuals are better equipped to navigate the challenges and setbacks that may arise during the debt payoff process.

In essence, "Creating an Effective Debt Payoff Plan: Mastering Debt Payoff" serves as a beacon of guidance for individuals navigating the often overwhelming terrain of debt. Souffrant's approach is both practical and empathetic, providing readers with the tools to not only craft a customized debt repayment strategy but also to foster a mindset that ensures long-term financial success. As readers engage with the insights and strategies presented, they embark on a transformative journey toward debt freedom, reclaiming control over their financial destiny and inching closer to the realization of true financial independence.

In the intricate landscape of personal finance, the chapter on "Tailoring the Plan to Your Financial Goals and Situation: Mastering Debt Payoff" from Jamila Souffrant's "Your Path to Financial Independence" emerges as a beacon, guiding readers through the nuanced process of crafting a debt payoff plan that is not only effective but deeply aligned with their unique financial circumstances and aspirations. This section of the guide serves as a personalized toolkit, empowering individuals to navigate the complex terrain of debt repayment with intentionality and purpose.

8.1 Aligning Debt Payoff with Individual Goals:

The journey begins by emphasizing the importance of aligning debt payoff efforts with individual financial goals. Souffrant encourages readers to define their aspirations, whether it's building an emergency fund, saving for a home, or investing in education. By anchoring the debt payoff plan within the broader context of personal goals, individuals cultivate a sense of purpose that fuels their commitment to the journey.

8.2 Adapting Strategies to Financial Situation:

Recognizing the diversity of financial situations, the chapter delves into the importance of adapting debt payoff strategies to individual circumstances. Souffrant provides insights into tailoring the plan based on income levels, family obligations, and other unique factors that shape financial realities. By acknowledging the specific challenges and opportunities inherent in each situation, readers gain a more nuanced and effective approach to debt repayment.

8.3 Customizing Repayment Methods:

Within the framework of the debt payoff plan, Souffrant explores the customization of repayment methods. The chapter guides readers through considerations such as the choice between the debt snowball and debt avalanche methods, helping individuals select an approach that resonates with their psychological preferences and aligns with their financial goals. This customization ensures that the chosen method serves as a powerful tool rather than a one-size-fits-all prescription.

8.4 Factoring in Lifestyle and Personal Values:

Beyond the numbers, Souffrant introduces the concept of factoring in lifestyle and personal values when tailoring a debt payoff plan. This holistic approach recognizes that financial decisions are intrinsically tied to one's lifestyle and values. By incorporating these elements into the plan, individuals not only enhance their financial well-being but also ensure that the journey toward debt freedom is personally fulfilling.

8.5 Establishing Realistic Milestones:

Setting realistic milestones is a cornerstone of an effective debt payoff plan. Souffrant guides readers through the process of establishing achievable goals, fostering a sense of accomplishment at each stage of the journey. By breaking down the overarching debt repayment goal into manageable milestones, individuals maintain motivation and celebrate progress along the way.

8.6 Integrating Long-Term Financial Planning:

The chapter concludes by highlighting the importance of integrating debt payoff efforts with long-term financial planning. Souffrant recognizes that debt is just one component of an individual's financial landscape. By considering how debt repayment fits into broader financial strategies, readers gain a comprehensive perspective that ensures sustained financial health beyond the immediate goal of debt freedom.

In essence, "Tailoring the Plan to Your Financial Goals and Situation: Mastering Debt Payoff" serves as a testament to the personalized and holistic approach advocated by Souffrant. This chapter is not a rigid set of rules but a flexible and empowering guide that invites individuals to actively shape their debt payoff journey in alignment with their unique circumstances and aspirations. As readers engage with the insights and strategies presented, they embark on a transformative process of mastering debt payoff— one that is not only effective but also deeply meaningful and personally fulfilling. Souffrant's approach transcends traditional financial advice, inviting readers to craft a debt repayment plan that becomes a seamless and purposeful part of their journey towards financial independence.

Achieving Financial Independence and Embracing Prosperity: Savoring Prosperity and Pleasure

In the culminating chapter of "Your Path to Financial Independence" by Jamila Souffrant, readers are ushered into the realm of fulfillment and abundance with the title "Achieving Financial Independence and Embracing Prosperity: Savoring Prosperity and Pleasure." This chapter serves not only as the crescendo of the financial journey but as a celebration of the efforts invested in mastering one's finances. Souffrant, with her insightful guidance, navigates readers through the transformative landscape of financial independence, encouraging them to savor the fruits of their labor and embrace a life rich in both prosperity and pleasure.

9.1 The Culmination of Financial Independence:

The journey towards financial independence culminates in this chapter, marking a pivotal moment of achievement and empowerment. Souffrant underscores the significance of this milestone, emphasizing that financial independence is not merely a destination but a transformative journey that empowers individuals to take control of their financial destiny.

9.2 The Intersection of Prosperity and Pleasure:

At the heart of the chapter lies the exploration of the intersection between prosperity and pleasure. Souffrant challenges the notion that financial independence is solely about frugality and sacrifice. Instead, she paints a vivid picture of a life where financial freedom coexists with pleasure, where individuals can savor the joys of life without compromising their long-term financial well-being.

9.3 Navigating the Shift in Mindset:

Souffrant delves into the importance of navigating a shift in mindset as individuals transition from the pursuit of financial independence to the actualization of prosperity. Readers are encouraged to release the scarcity mindset that may have fueled their journey, embracing a mindset of abundance and gratitude. This shift lays the foundation for a life that is not just financially secure but also emotionally and spiritually fulfilling.

9.4 Cultivating a Sustainable Lifestyle:

The chapter guides readers through the process of cultivating a sustainable lifestyle post-financial independence. Souffrant introduces the concept of intentional living, where choices and expenditures are aligned with personal values and bring lasting joy. This intentional approach ensures that the newfound prosperity is not squandered but becomes a source of sustained fulfillment.

9.5 Balancing Present Pleasure with Future Security:

While celebrating the pleasures of the present, Souffrant offers insights into the delicate art of balancing immediate gratification with future security. Readers learn to savor the pleasures of life without jeopardizing the financial foundations they've worked hard to establish. This balance is portrayed as the key to a life that is both joyful and secure.

9.6 Giving Back and Impacting Others:

The chapter concludes with a call to give back and impact others positively. Souffrant highlights the profound fulfillment that comes from contributing to the well-being of others, whether through charitable endeavors, mentorship, or community engagement. This aspect of the journey transcends personal prosperity, extending the benefits of financial independence to the broader community.

In essence, "Achieving Financial Independence and Embracing Prosperity: Savoring Prosperity and Pleasure" is not just a conclusion but an invitation—a call to embrace a life that is abundant, purposeful, and joyous. Souffrant's approach is a testament to the idea that financial independence is not a solitary pursuit but a gateway to a life where prosperity and pleasure coalesce. As readers engage with the insights and strategies presented, they are empowered not only to savor the fruits of financial independence but to cultivate a life that resonates with their deepest values and aspirations. Souffrant's guidance transcends traditional financial advice, transforming the pursuit of financial independence into a holistic and fulfilling journey towards a future rich in prosperity and pleasure.

In the concluding chapter of "Your Path to Financial Independence," Jamila Souffrant brings readers to the intersection of financial wisdom and personal enjoyment with the chapter titled "Balancing Responsible Saving with Enjoyable Spending: Savoring Prosperity and Pleasure." This segment serves as a guiding light for individuals who have achieved financial independence, inviting them to navigate the delicate dance between responsible saving and the enjoyment of life's pleasures. Souffrant's insightful approach encourages readers to savor the prosperity they've diligently worked towards without compromising the essence of a fulfilling and joyful life.

10.1 Embracing the Rewards of Responsible Saving:

The journey begins by celebrating the rewards of responsible saving. Souffrant acknowledges the discipline and commitment that have led individuals to financial independence. Readers are encouraged to appreciate the fruits of their savings journey, recognizing that financial responsibility is not only about securing the future but also about creating opportunities for present enjoyment.

10.2 Challenging the Dichotomy of Saving vs. Spending:

In this chapter, Souffrant challenges the conventional dichotomy of saving versus spending. Rather than viewing these two actions as opposing forces, she invites readers to see them as complementary elements in the quest for a balanced and prosperous life. By breaking down the perceived barriers between saving and spending, individuals can forge a path that harmonizes financial prudence with the enjoyment of life's pleasures.

10.3 Defining Enjoyable Spending:

Central to the chapter is the exploration of enjoyable spending. Souffrant encourages readers to reflect on what brings them true joy and fulfillment. Whether it's travel, experiences, hobbies, or simply indulging in small luxuries, individuals are prompted to identify and embrace the aspects of life that contribute to their overall well-being. This personalized approach to enjoyable spending ensures that each expenditure aligns with individual values and brings genuine satisfaction.

10.4 Creating a Joy-Centric Budget:

Souffrant introduces the concept of a joy-centric budget, where financial decisions are guided by the pursuit of happiness and fulfillment. Readers learn to allocate resources intentionally, ensuring that each dollar spent contributes to a sense of joy and satisfaction. This transformative shift from a restrictive budget to a joy-centric budget empowers individuals to make conscious and meaningful spending choices.

10.5 Mitigating Guilt and Embracing Pleasure:

Many individuals, even after achieving financial independence, may grapple with feelings of guilt associated with spending on non-essential items. Souffrant addresses this common dilemma by encouraging readers to mitigate guilt and embrace pleasure. By reframing the narrative around spending, individuals can cultivate a positive and guilt-free relationship with their financial choices, fostering a healthier mindset towards enjoyment.

10.6 The Art of Mindful Spending:

The chapter concludes with an exploration of the art of mindful spending. Souffrant guides readers to cultivate a heightened awareness of their spending decisions, encouraging them to question whether each expenditure aligns with their values and brings authentic joy. Through mindfulness, individuals can navigate the fine balance between saving and spending, ensuring that each financial choice contributes to a life that is both prosperous and pleasurable.

In essence, "Balancing Responsible Saving with Enjoyable Spending: Savoring Prosperity and Pleasure" is a transformative guide that transcends traditional notions of financial management. Souffrant's approach goes beyond the numbers, inviting individuals to embrace a holistic and joy-centric perspective on their financial journey. As readers engage with the insights and strategies presented, they embark on a path that celebrates the rewards of responsible saving while savoring the pleasures of life. This chapter serves as a compass, guiding individuals towards a future where financial prosperity and personal enjoyment coalesce, creating a life that is not only financially secure but also deeply fulfilling and rich in pleasure.

In the culminating chapter of "Your Path to Financial Independence," Jamila Souffrant offers readers a profound exploration into the art of intentional living with the title "Cultivating a Lifestyle that Brings Joy and Fulfillment: Savoring Prosperity and Pleasure." This pivotal section of the guide serves as a blueprint for individuals who have attained financial independence, guiding them to transcend mere financial success and embrace a lifestyle that aligns with their deepest values, bringing enduring joy and fulfillment.

11.1 The Essence of Intentional Living:

The chapter begins by delving into the essence of intentional living. Souffrant encourages readers to shift their focus from passive existence to purposeful engagement with life. Intentional living is presented as a conscious choice to align one's actions, values, and expenditures with a vision of a life that brings authentic joy and fulfillment.

11.2 Identifying Core Values and Priorities:

Central to the cultivation of a joy-centric lifestyle is the identification of core values and priorities. Souffrant prompts readers to reflect deeply on what truly matters to them. Whether it's relationships, personal growth, experiences, or contributing to others, individuals are guided to distill their values and priorities, laying the foundation for a life that resonates with purpose and satisfaction.

11.3 Crafting a Lifestyle Blueprint:

The chapter unfolds into the practical application of intentional living through the crafting of a lifestyle blueprint. Souffrant introduces readers to the concept of creating a personalized plan that outlines the desired elements of their lives. From daily habits to significant life choices, the lifestyle blueprint becomes a roadmap for individuals to navigate towards a future that reflects their unique aspirations and values.

11.4 Allocating Resources According to Values:

Intentional living extends to the allocation of resources, both time and money, according to one's values. Souffrant emphasizes the importance of aligning financial decisions with the identified values and priorities. By consciously directing resources towards what truly matters, individuals create a life that is not only financially sound but also deeply meaningful.

11.5 Embracing Minimalism and Purposeful Consumption:

The chapter explores the liberating concept of minimalism and purposeful consumption. Souffrant advocates for a mindful approach to possessions, encouraging readers to declutter their lives of unnecessary belongings. By embracing minimalism, individuals create space for what truly brings joy and meaning, fostering a lifestyle that is unburdened by excessive materialism.

11.6 Navigating Challenges and Cultivating Resilience:

Souffrant acknowledges that the path to intentional living is not without challenges. The chapter provides insights into navigating obstacles and cultivating resilience. Whether facing external pressures or internal doubts, readers are guided to stay true to their values and priorities, fostering a resilient mindset that propels them forward on their journey towards a fulfilling lifestyle.

11.7 Fostering Connection and Contribution:

The exploration of intentional living concludes with a focus on fostering connection and contribution. Souffrant highlights the significance of building meaningful relationships and contributing positively to the community. By embracing connection and contribution, individuals create a web of support and purpose that enhances the richness of their lives.

In essence, "Cultivating a Lifestyle that Brings Joy and Fulfillment: Savoring Prosperity and Pleasure" is a transformative guide that transcends conventional notions of success and prosperity. Souffrant's approach invites individuals to not only savor the financial rewards of their journey but to intentionally shape a life that resonates with joy and fulfillment. As readers engage with the insights and strategies presented, they embark on a profound journey towards intentional living—a life that reflects their deepest values, prioritizes joy, and serves as a testament to the true essence of prosperity and pleasure. This chapter becomes a guiding beacon, empowering individuals to craft a lifestyle that is not just prosperous but profoundly meaningful.

CONCLUSION

In the concluding chapter of "Your Path to Financial Independence," Jamila Souffrant leaves readers with a resonant message that transcends the confines of traditional financial guides. The journey embarked upon within the pages of this book extends far beyond the realm of budgeting, saving, and investing. It is a transformative odyssey that invites individuals to redefine their relationship with money, empowering them to shape a life that is not merely financially secure but deeply fulfilling.

The essence of financial independence, as Souffrant beautifully articulates, lies in the delicate balance between responsible saving and joyful spending. It's a dance that requires mindfulness, intentionality, and a keen understanding of one's values and priorities. The book serves as a comprehensive guide, navigating readers through the complexities of debt, savings, and investments while emphasizing the importance of aligning financial decisions with personal aspirations.

As readers progress through the stages of their financial journey, Souffrant gently guides them to confront not only the numerical aspects of wealth but also the emotional and psychological dimensions of money. The five Journeyer stages become not just markers of progress but tools for self-discovery, prompting individuals to assess their values, goals, and desires in the pursuit of a life that is authentically their own.

The transformative power of intentional living takes center stage in the concluding chapters, urging readers to craft a lifestyle that brings enduring joy and fulfillment. Souffrant's insights into minimalism, purposeful consumption, and fostering connections create a roadmap for individuals to navigate the complexities of a world often dominated by materialism and external pressures.

Ultimately, "Your Path to Financial Independence" transcends the realm of personal finance literature, becoming a manifesto for intentional and purposeful living. It is an invitation to savor the prosperity and pleasure earned through financial independence while navigating the delicate dance between saving and spending. Souffrant's approach is not just about the numbers; it's about crafting a life that aligns with one's values, priorities, and aspirations.

As readers close the final chapter, they are not just equipped with financial tools but armed with a profound understanding of themselves and a vision for a life that goes beyond financial metrics. "Your Path to Financial Independence" becomes a guiding light, empowering individuals not only to achieve financial freedom but to savor the richness of a life well-lived—one that is prosperous, pleasurable, and deeply fulfilling.

www.ingramcontent.com/pod-product-compliance
Lightning Source LLC
Chambersburg PA
CBHW050053260726
48658CB00005B/1922